C000179160

MEMENTO MORI

CHURCHES AND CHURCHYARDS OF ENGLAND

MEMENTO

A PERSONAL SELECTION BY
Simon Marsden

MORI

CHURCHES AND CHURCHYARDS OF ENGLAND

ENGLISH HERITAGE

'WHILE I THOUGHT THAT I WAS LEARNING HOW TO LIVE,
I HAVE BEEN LEARNING HOW TO DIE.'

Leonardo da Vinci, 1452–1519

INTRODUCTION *by* SIR SIMON MARSDEN

When a Roman general paraded his troops through the streets of the capital celebrating a great victory, standing behind him in his chariot would be one of his slaves, whose task was to remind his master that, although this day was a great triumph, tomorrow might be different – for despite his power and fame the victor was merely mortal. Hence the meaning of the Latin words *memento mori* – remember you will die. Throughout history similar examples of this warning can be found in the funereal art and architecture of the many different cultures of our world as a reminder of man's fragile destiny. Perhaps the most powerful are the cadaver tombs portraying the skeletal corpse of the deceased, and the medieval church paintings known as the *Danse Macabre*, depicting the Grim Reaper carrying off rich and poor alike. In Renaissance times a human skull, or an hour glass on the poet's desk, became a striking symbol of life's uncertainty, and it was fashionable to wear jewellery with a death motif. Mary Queen of Scots owned an ornate watch carved in the form of a silver skull, embellished with lines from the Roman philosopher and poet Horace.

But this book is intended as more than just a reminder of the inevitability of our impending death. For the many churches and churchyards portrayed here lie at the very heart of our villages, towns and cities, and are central to our history and culture. It is here that many of us are not only baptised, married and eventually laid to rest, but where we also discover spiritual inspiration and refuge amongst their many architectural masterpieces: the memorials, effigies and stained glass created by some of Europe's greatest sculptors and artists throughout the ages. Inevitably, with the almost endless number of impressive churches and monuments in England, the content of the book could only ever be my personal choice and it does not cover the whole of the country, or indeed every aspect of the subject matter. The final selection and order of images is also an emotional, visual response rather than an ordered anthology – in short the images reflect what I feel. The text is simply intended to supplement these images, in the form of poetry, prose, anecdotes and epitaphs.

Sadly, in the present age, many of our churches are under threat as religious congregations decline, and many of these traditional sanctuaries are now permanently locked to preserve their valuable contents from thieves and vandals. Alarms and CCTV cameras are attached to the walls where classical statues and medieval saints once stared down. Finding the key can be an adventure in itself but, once you pass through the threshold of the ancient wooden door, peace and tranquility surround and envelop you. In the often dark, shadowy interiors the reflection of the sun through stained-glass windows lights up the faces of the alabaster or marble effigies that lie staring up at the heavens. Resembling spirits frozen in time, they seem to be waiting like *Sleeping Beauty* or the legendary *King Arthur* for the embrace of a saviour to awaken them – but who never comes.

Occasionally, I would meet an old lady polishing the brasses or arranging flowers while I photographed. Who, I often wondered, would do their job in future years? And the congregation – would they simply be ghosts too? In one particular churchyard I was joined by an old man as I was packing away my cameras in the failing light. He had come to lock up the church as he said he had done almost every evening for the last seven years since his wife's sudden death. He was frail and his clothes were worn but he had a sympathetic expression that portrayed a certain calm, an aura of peace. He told me that this simple task, that he had inherited from his wife, had given him a purpose, the will to go on in spite of his loneliness.

Through my work as a photographer I have spent many hours alone in search of my own particular truth, whether within the ivy-clad walls and dark passageways of a gothic ruin, or amongst the broken tombs of an overgrown graveyard. It is here that I have always found a stillness, a peace that inspires my soul and reminds me of my childhood in a remote part of the Lincolnshire Wolds. I was raised as a Catholic and attended a Benedictine boarding school from a young age, where I soon rebelled against the rigid conformity of its regime, but never lost the sense of spirituality and fantasy that this environment transfused in me. Perhaps because of this mystical awakening I have always felt myself to be somewhat of an outsider, an observer, with little interest in the automation and insensitivity of our everyday mundane existence, believing that there is another more meaningful dimension to life.

In this uncertain age, where the difference between right and wrong is no longer clear, we appear to live in a constant state of change. What is certain is that many of our historic churches now lie empty and derelict, their graveyards overgrown and their magnificent works of art in decay. They have fallen victim to a decline in organised religion, lack of funds and general neglect, and this major part of our heritage is now at risk of being lost forever. There are those who say that the church and its teachings are out of touch with reality, and that these buildings no longer serve any purpose today. These same people would burn or sell the pews to make their interiors functional, turning them into antique markets, craft shops or even building societies. But then, I wonder, where will we find a place of refuge from this stressful world we have created, a sanctuary in which we can reflect on the mystery and fragility of our existence? There is a strange beauty in Death and his singular role as a guardian of secrets, and our churches are where we prepare ourselves for this inevitable day of reckoning. The enigma is answered at the point of our demise, by the transparency of our lives.

Sir Simon Marsden, August 2007

IN AFFECTIONATE

**Stained glass,
All Saints Church,
Bishop Burton,
East Yorkshire**

'MY FATHER'S EYES had closed upon the light of this world six months, when mine opened on it. There is something strange to me, even now, in the reflection that he never saw me; and something stranger yet in the shadowy remembrance that I have of my first childish associations with his white grave-stone in the churchyard, and of the indefinable compassion I used to feel for it lying out alone there in the dark night, when our little parlour was warm and bright with fire and candle, and the doors of our house were – almost cruelly, it seemed to me sometimes – bolted and locked against it.'

From DAVID COPPERFIELD *by* Charles Dickens, 1812–70

'...IT PAINED ME TO THINK OF THE DEAR OLD PLACE as altogether abandoned; of the weeds growing tall in the garden, and the fallen leaves lying thick and wet upon the paths. I imagined how the winds of winter would howl round it, how the cold rain would beat upon the window-glass, how the moon would make ghosts on the walls of the empty rooms, watching their solitude all night. I thought afresh of the grave in the churchyard, underneath the tree: and it seemed as if the house were dead too, now, and all connected with my father and mother were faded away.'

From DAVID COPPERFIELD *by* Charles Dickens, 1812–70

Tomb of Charles Sackville,
5th Duke of Dorset, who died in 1843.
St Peter's Church, Lowick,
Northamptonshire

21

THE GREAT 19TH-CENTURY ROMANTIC POET Lord Byron (1788–1824) inherited his semi-derelict ancestral home Newstead Abbey after graduating from Cambridge in 1808. The crumbling gothic mansion was a perfect muse for his decadent imagination, and suited his scandalous lifestyle – particularly after he converted the former Prior's lodgings, a reputedly haunted chamber, into a grandiose bedroom where he indulged in his many amorous adventures. One of the few building works he carried out on the estate was a monumental tomb to his beloved Newfoundland dog, *Boatswain*, who died of rabies. He interred the dog in a vault on the site of the high altar of the ancient abbey, with instructions that on his own death he should be buried alongside probably the most constant friend he had had in his tumultuous life. But his wish was not granted and his remains were laid to rest in the family vault at nearby Hucknall parish church.

His moving and lengthy epitaph to *Boatswain* ends with the words:

'To mark a friend's remains these stones arise,
I never knew but one and here he lies.'

'DEATH IS THE VEIL WHICH THOSE WHO LIVE CALL LIFE:
THEY SLEEP AND IT IS LIFTED.'

From PROMETHEUS UNBOUND, ACT 3, SCENE 3 *by* Percy Bysshe Shelley, 1792–1822

'Angel of Doom' monument, the Lancaster tomb, East Sheen Cemetery, London

MY LOVE, SHE SLEEPS! Oh, may her sleep,
As it is lasting, so be deep!
Soft may the worms about her creep!
Far in the forest, dim and old,
For her may some tall vault unfold –
Some vault that oft hath flung its black
And winged panels fluttering back,
Triumphant, o'er the crested palls,
Of her grand family funerals –
Some sepulchre, remote, alone,
Against whose portal she hath thrown,
In childhood, many an idle stone –
Some tomb from out whose sounding door
She ne'er shall force an echo more,
Thrilling to think, poor child of sin!
It was the dead who groaned within.

From THE SLEEPER *by* Edgar Allan Poe, 1809–49

THIS FINE MEMORIAL IS THE LAST WORK of the French sculptor Louis François Roubiliac (1702–62), famous for his monuments of Handel in London and Newton in Cambridge. It was commissioned at a cost of £500 by Ann Bellamy to commemorate the life of her husband George Lynn of Southwick Hall. A notable astronomer and antiquary, Lynn set up a 13ft (4m) telescope to observe the eclipses of Jupiter's satellites in the years 1724 to 1726.

One of his ancestors, also called George Lynn, was one of the eight banderole-bearers at the funeral of Mary Queen of Scots after her execution at Fotheringhay Castle in 1587. There is a legend that the burial certificate is walled up somewhere in Southwick Hall.

INFANTS' GRAVES are steps of angels, where

Earth's brightest gems of innocence repose.

God is their parent, and they need no tear,

He takes them to His bosom from earth's woes,

A bud their lifetime and a flower their close.

Their spirits are an Iris of the skies,

Needing no prayers; a sunset's happy close,

Gone are the bright rays of their soft blue eyes;

Flowers weep in dewdrops o'er them, and the gale gently sighs.

Their lives were nothing but a sunny shower,

Melting on flowers as tears melt from the eye.

Their deaths were dewdrops on heaven's amaranth bower,

And tolled on flowers as summer gales went by.

They bowed and trembled, yet they left no sigh,

And the sun smiled to show their end was well.

Infants have naught to weep for ere they die;

All prayers are needless, beads they need not tell,

White flowers their mourners are, nature their passing-bell.

GRAVES OF INFANTS *by* John Clare, 1793–1864

'NIGHT, LIKE A GIANT, fills the church, from pavement to roof, and holds dominion through the silent hours. Pale dawn again comes peeping through the windows: and, giving place to day, sees night withdraw into the vaults, and follows it, and drives it out, and hides among the dead.'

From DOMBEY AND SON *by* Charles Dickens, 1812–70

'IT WAS A VERY AGED GHOSTLY PLACE; the church had been built many hundreds of years ago, and had once had a convent or monastery attached; for arches in ruins, remains of oriel windows, and fragments of blackened walls, were yet standing, while other portions of the old building, which had crumbled away and fallen down, were mingled with the churchyard earth and overgrown with grass, as if they too claimed a burying-place and sought to mix their ashes with the dust of men.'

From THE OLD CURIOSITY SHOP *by* Charles Dickens, 1812–70

**Mausoleum of Andrew Ducrow,
Kensal Green Cemetery, London**

Said to have been 'erected by genius for the reception of its own remains', this fantastic Greco-Egyptian mausoleum contains the body of the famous circus owner and equestrian performer Andrew Ducrow (1793–1842). One of his most popular stunts was the 'The Courier of St Petersburg' which involved him controlling five galloping horses while standing on the backs of two of them. His gloves and ringmaster's hat, carved in stone, lie nearby.

HERE RLPO...
IN SACRED M...
THE MORTA R MA...
MARGARET DUC...
THE BELOVED W...
DREW DUCROW, ...
M THI MONUMENT ...
HIS ROFE ... IN
LIFE JANUA T I...
IT IT HEAVENE...
CAN IN M...
ILL NOW TH...
PIRO FEL...

HAS FO...
WH...

FATHER
HE HEARTYO F...
VLD AND LANE IT...
TO OD WHO CKV...
TEMBER 1873...
N HIS AGE...

MEMORY OF...

AGED 88 YEARS...

Because I could not stop for Death —
He kindly stopped for me —
The carriage held but just Ourselves —
And Immortality.

We slowly drove — He knew no haste
And I had put away
My labour and my leisure too,
For his Civility.

We passed the School, where Children strove
At Recess — in the Ring —
We passed the Fields of Gazing Grain —
We passed the Setting Sun —

Or rather — He passed us —
The Dews drew quivering and chill —
For only Gossamer, my Gown —
My Tippet — only Tulle.

We paused before a House that seemed
A Swelling of the Ground —
The Roof was scarcely visible —
The Cornice — in the Ground.

Since then —'tis Centuries — and yet
Feels shorter than the Day
I first surmised the Horses' Heads
Were toward Eternity.

Because I Could Not Stop for Death *by* Emily Dickinson, 1830–86

Effigies of William Pope, Earl of Downe,
and his wife, with below one of the
couple's grieving daughters,
All Saints Church, Wroxton, Oxfordshire

'OH, FOR THE TIME
WHEN I SHALL SLEEP
WITHOUT IDENTITY...'

From THE PHILOSOPHER *by* Emily Brontë, 1818–48

ALL THAT NOW REMAINS OF THE VILLAGE OF Wolterton is the ancient round tower of St Margaret's Church that is believed to date from Saxon times. It stands in the parkland of the Wolterton estate where Horatio Walpole, younger brother of Sir Robert Walpole the Prime Minister, built the present Hall in the 1720s. Twenty years later the village was reduced to only a few houses and the church had begun to fall into ruin. According to church records the last burial took place in 1747 and the last marriage in 1772.

Victorian stories claimed the tombstones from the graveyard of St Margaret's were sold by Horatio's grandson, the 2nd Earl of Orford, and that the ghost of a member of one local family, the Scamblers, who were buried in the chancel, haunts the church tower searching for the tombs of her relatives. This troubled spirit had to be placated at the funerals of the Earls of Orford by driving the body three times round the tower before being buried at nearby Wickmere church.

50 **Effigy of a member of the
Poole family, Church of St Kenelm,
Sapperton, Gloucestershire**

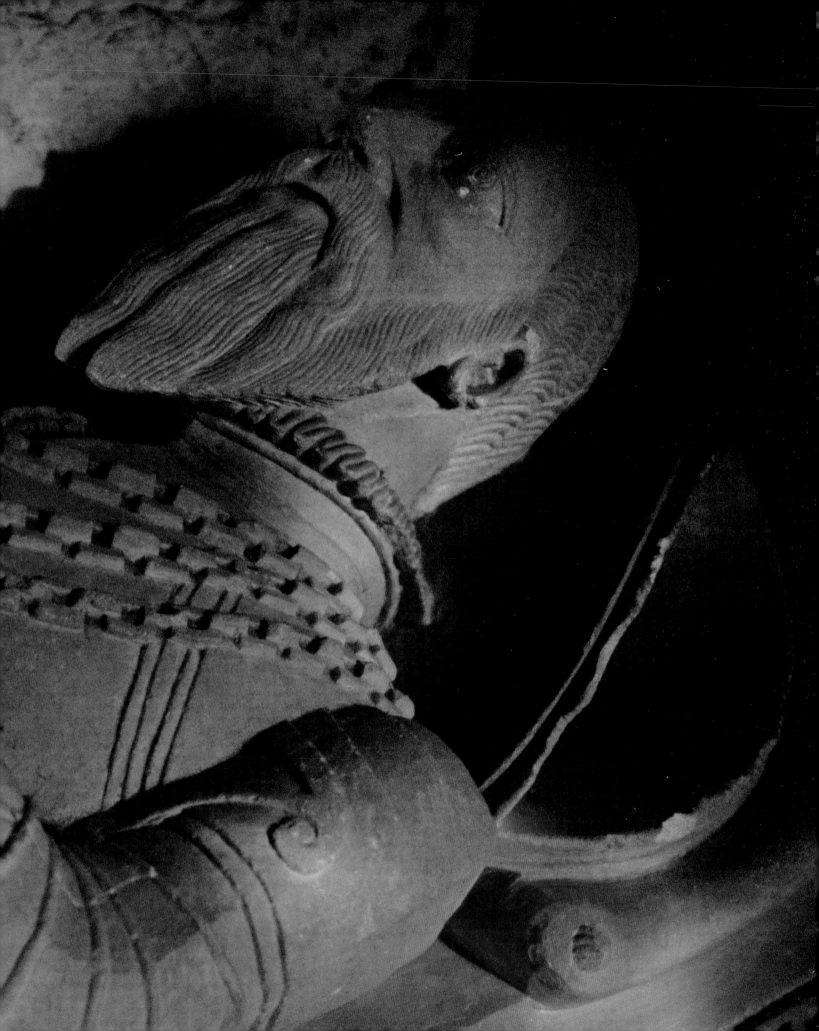

L YING CLOSE TO THE ALTAR STEPS THIS SENSATIONAL memorial was designed in 1775 by Robert Adam (1728–92) with sculpture by Peter Matthias van Gelder (1739–1809). The circular sepulchre is decorated in the ancient Ionic order with the urn in the centre containing the ashes of the deceased. The figure seated by the pedestal represents the dying duchess while the statue of a woman holding a babe by the hand symbolises widows and children mourning for the loss of a great benefactor. The figure on the left represents an angel pointing to a heavenly reward.

'FOR THE NIGHT-WIND has a dismal
trick of wandering round and round a
building of that sort, and moaning as it
goes; and of trying, with its hand, the
windows and the doors; and seeking out
some crevices by which to enter. And
when it has gone in; as one not finding
what it seeks, whatever that may be, it
wails and howls to issue forth again:
and not content with stalking through
the aisles, and gliding round and round
the pillars, and tempting the deep
organ, soars up to the roof, and strives
to rend the rafters: then flings itself
despairingly upon the stones below, and
passes, muttering, into the vaults.'

From THE CHIMES: A GOBLIN STORY *by* Charles Dickens, 1812–70

Detail from a tomb, Brompton Cemetery, London below
Effigy of William Harry Vane, 1st Duke of Cleveland, St Mary's Church, Staindrop, Co Durham opposite

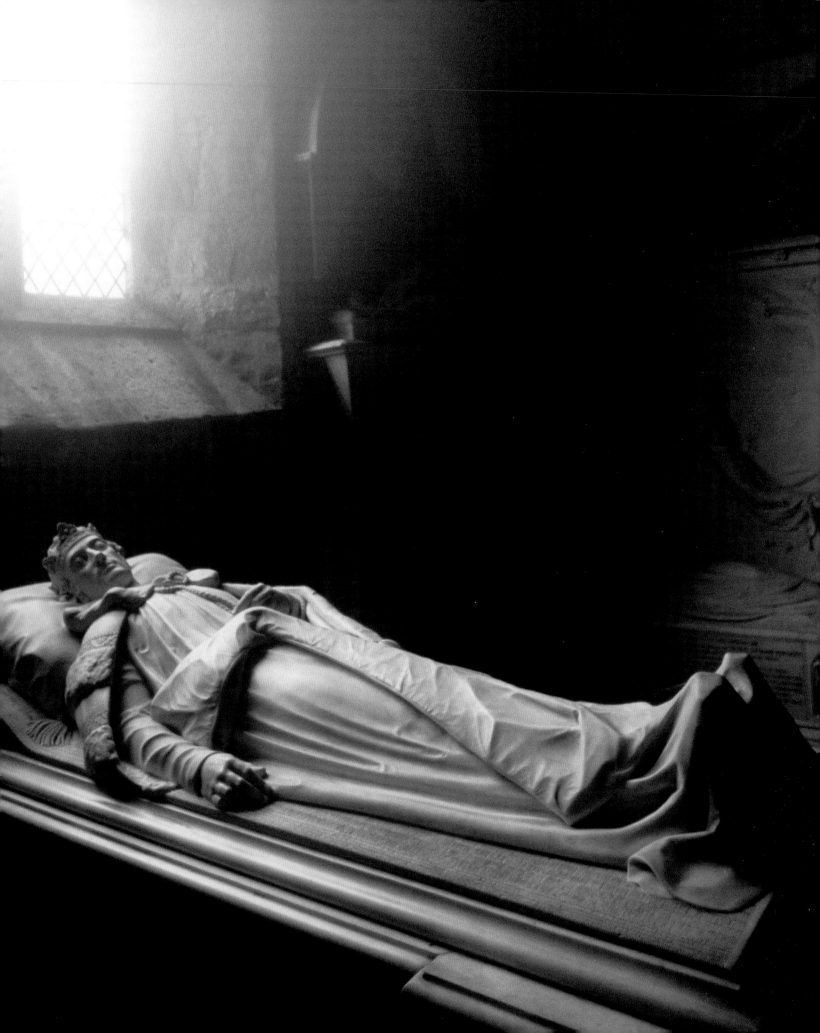

A STRANGE VOLCANIC ROCK FORMATION TOWERS over the village of Roche on Bodmin Moor. On its summit stands an ancient chapel dedicated to Saint Michael in 1409, and below its crumbling walls there was once a hermitage. This cell is said to have been the final retreat of a rich man in the 15th century – he had contracted leprosy and, rather than risk infecting his family with the deadly disease, he exiled himself on the isolated rock. However, his daughter, Gundred, refused to accept her father's brave sacrifice and followed him to tend his terrible affliction. She regularly bathed his sores with water from the nearby well which now bears her name.

Even today the visitor feels a certain apprehension on approaching this geological phenomenon. It has a truly sinister aura and it is not surprising that over the centuries it has been the focus of many myths and legends. The rocks are said to be the haunt of the legendary Jan Tregeagle, an evil 17th-century magistrate who sold his soul to the devil. He tried to gain sanctuary in the chapel when chased by a pack of hell-hounds across the moor, and his ghost can still be seen attempting to climb through a window of the ruins. Another story claims that the tragic lovers Tristan and Isolde sought refuge here while fleeing from her husband.

'THE BOAST OF HERALDRY, THE POMP OF POWER,
AND ALL THAT BEAUTY, ALL THAT WEALTH E'ER GAVE,
AWAITS ALIKE TH'INEVITABLE HOUR:
THE PATHS OF GLORY LEAD BUT TO THE GRAVE.'

From ELEGY WRITTEN IN A COUNTRY CHURCHYARD *by* Thomas Gray, 1716–71

St Helen's Church, Biscathorpe, Lincolnshire

'THE COLD HOARFROST GLISTENED on the tombstones, and sparkled like rows of gems, among the stone carvings of the old church. The snow lay hard and crisp upon the ground, and spread over the thickly-strewn mounds of earth, so white and smooth a cover, that it seemed as if corpses lay there, hidden only by their winding sheets.'

From THE STORY OF THE GOBLINS WHO STOLE A SEXTON in THE POSTHUMOUS PAPERS OF THE PICKWICK CLUB *by* Charles Dickens, 1812–70

**Statues of King Lud and his two sons,
St Dunstan-in-the-West, Fleet Street,
City of London**

IN A DARK NICHE OF THE VESTRY PORCH OF St Dunstan's stand three decaying statues hidden from the light of day. Originally part of the old west gate of the City of London known as Ludgate, these mysterious figures are King Lud and his two sons Androgeus and Tenvantius, who have had several resting places since the landmark was demolished in 1760. According to Geoffrey of Monmouth's legendary *History of the Kings of Britain*, Lud was a king of Britain in pre-Roman times, and his reign was notable for the building of cities and the refortification of Trinovantum (London), which he was especially fond of. Geoffrey explains that the name London derives from *Caer Lud* meaning Lud's City.

I DIED FOR BEAUTY, BUT WAS SCARCE
ADJUSTED IN THE TOMB,
WHEN ONE WHO DIED FOR TRUTH WAS LAIN
IN AN ADJOINING ROOM.

HE QUESTIONED SOFTLY WHY I FAILED?
"FOR BEAUTY," I REPLIED.
"AND I FOR TRUTH, THE TWO ARE ONE;
WE BRETHREN ARE," HE SAID.

AND SO, AS KINSMAN MET A NIGHT,
WE TALKED BETWEEN THE ROOMS,
UNTIL THE MOSS HAD REACHED OUR LIPS,
AND COVERED UP OUR NAMES.

I DIED FOR BEAUTY *by* Emily Dickinson, 1830–86

**Wall monument to James Vaulx and family,
St Mary's Church, Meysey Hampton, Gloucestershire**

ELIEVED TO HAVE BEEN BUILT BY THE
Knights Templars in the 13th century the small,
atmospheric church of St Mary contains an elabo-
rate and striking 17th-century monument in painted stone
to the physician James Vaulx, his two wives and 14 children.

Translated from the old English the epitaph reads:

Stay, mortal, stay: and look upon
The language of a speaking stone;
Nor wonder if it be, that he should give
Speech to a stone; who let men live;
When nature bid them die; it is he
By whom I live; not he by me.
This said; I may again be dumb
I've spoke enough to tell whose tomb
This is: and thou may grieving know,
That none but Vaulx can lie below.

St Cecilia – patron saint of musicians – St Lawrence's Church,
Lechlade, Gloucestershire below
Detail from stained-glass window, All Saints Church,
Bishop Burton, East Yorkshire opposite

75

'At the great iron gate of the
churchyard he stopped and looked in.
He looked up at the high tower spectrally
resisting the wind, and he looked round at
the white tombstones, like enough to the
dead in their winding-sheets, and he
counted the nine tolls of the clock-bell.'

From Our Mutual Friend *by* Charles Dickens, 1812–70

'"It is a sensation not experienced by many mortals," said he, "to be looking into a churchyard on a wild windy night, and to feel that I no more hold a place among the living than these dead do, and even to know that I lie buried somewhere else, as they lie buried here. Nothing uses me to it. A spirit that was once a man could hardly feel stranger or lonelier, going unrecognized among mankind, than I feel."'

From Our Mutual Friend *by* Charles Dickens, 1812–70

80   **Tomb, St Andrew's churchyard,
      Fulletby, Lincolnshire**

The Garden by the Graveyard

'WE HAD A GARDEN AT THE BACK OF THE house, not large, but with lawn, flowers, and a few trees. In daylight the trees leaned out over the churchyard or over the path through it and the stones were nothing but stones. But as the sun went down behind the church tower, the stones became stiller than stone – as if they were waiting. When the sun had gone down I did not look at the churchyard at all. I knew how the stones were lengthening, lifting and peering blankly, inscrutably, over the wall. As I went indoors, if I dared a backward glance, or climbed towards the little shot window, I saw how they did indeed peer; but up, always over my shoulder or my head, crowded, still, other. Then I would go quickly to my father or my mother or my brother for human company by the fire.

One afternoon I was sitting on the wall that divided our garden from the churchyard. Eight, was I, perhaps, or nine? Or older even? There is nothing by which I can tell. I contemplated the stones a few feet away and saw suddenly that several of them were flat up against our wall. I remember knowing then that I had seen and thought enough. My nights were miserable as it was, with every sort of apprehension given a label, and these even so only outliers of a central, not-comprehended dark. But the sun shone on the wall and I watched the inside of my head go on and take step after logical step. At which end of the grave does a stone stand? I remembered the sexton, Mr

Baker, calling them headstones and I made the final deduction that the dead lay, their heads under our wall, the rest of them projecting from their own place into our garden, their feet, their knees even, tucked under our lawn.

Logic is insistent. I recall an awareness at that moment that I was being foolish; that the demonstration of this proposition would do no one any good and me a great deal of harm. The lawn, almost the only uncontaminated place in the ancient neighbourhood, had been sunny and innocent until my deliberate exercise of logic had invited the enemy in.

What was this enemy? I cannot tell. He came with darkness and he reduced me to a shuddering terror that was incurable because it was indescribable. In daylight I thought of the Roman remains that had been dug up under the church as the oldest things near, sane things from sane people like myself. But at night, the Norman door and pillar, even the flint wall of our cellar, were older, far older, were rooted in the darkness under the earth.

How could I talk to (my parents) about darkness and the irrational? They knew so much, had such certainties, were backing all the obvious winners. I floated in their

world, holding on to a casual hand, sometimes sinking again in the dark. Then I found Edgar Allan Poe's *Tales of Mystery and Imagination.* I read them with a sort of shackled fascination and recognized their quality, knew they were reports, knew that he and I had been in the same place.

But my career was to be a scientific one. Science was very busy clearing up the universe. There was no place in this exquisitely logical universe for the terrors of darkness. There was darkness, of course, but it was just darkness, the absence of light; had none of the looming terror which I knew night-long in my very bones. God might have been a help but we had thrown Him out, along with Imperialism, Toryism, the Exploitation of Women, War and the Church of England. I nodded agreement, was precocious with the catchphrases of progress; but even in daylight now, the dead under the wall drew up the green coverlet of our grass and lay back with a heart-squeezing grin. Though cosmology was driving away the shadows of our ignorance, though bones were exhibited under glass, though the march of science was irresistible, its path did not lie through my particular darkness.'

From THE LADDER AND THE TREE in THE HOT GATES
by William Golding, 1911–93

'PEOPLE DO NOT DIE FOR US
IMMEDIATELY, BUT REMAIN
BATHED IN A SORT OF AURA
OF LIFE WHICH BEARS NO
RELATION TO TRUE
IMMORTALITY BUT THROUGH
WHICH THEY CONTINUE TO
OCCUPY OUR THOUGHTS IN
THE SAME WAY AS WHEN
THEY WERE ALIVE. IT IS AS
THOUGH THEY WERE
TRAVELLING ABROAD.'

Marcel Proust, 1871–1922

DUNWICH, AT ONE TIME THE ANCIENT CAPITAL of East Anglia, boasted eight churches, a bishop's palace, a mayor's mansion and ancient bronze gates of an immense size.

A few houses for the fishermen, a church, the eerie ruins of a priory and a leper hospital are all that now remain after 700 years of coastal erosion. During a great storm in 1328 the city was engulfed by the sea and old Dunwich now lies beneath the ever-advancing waves. The empty, eerie atmosphere has inspired many ghost stories including the terrifying *Whistle and I'll Come to You* by the English master of the genre M R James. Legend tells that the toll of phantom church bells can be heard from the watery depths, and latter-day Dunwich is unique in that the living mix openly with the dead, for along the clifftops skeletons can be seen protruding from their graves as the sea advances on the old graveyards. The mystical poet Swinburne immortalised this in verse:

Naked, shamed, cast out of consecration,
    Corpse and coffin, yea the very graves,
Scoffed at, scattered, shaken from their station,
    Spurned and scourged of wind and sea like slaves,
Desolate beyond man's desolation,
    Shrink and sink into the waste of waves.

Tombs, with bare white piteous bones protruded,
    Shroudless, down the loose collapsing banks,
Crumble, from their constant place detruded,
    That the sea devours and gives not thanks.
Graves where hope and prayer and sorrow brooded
    Gape and slide and perish, ranks on ranks.

From BY THE NORTH SEA *by* Algernon Charles Swinburne, 1837–1909

90 **Fifteenth-century effigy
of Sir Thomas Wykeham,
St Mary's Church,
Broughton, Oxfordshire**

Tomb of Ninon Michaelis, Kensal Green Cemetery, London

I AM NOT RESIGNED to the shutting away of loving hearts in the hard ground.
So it is, and so it will be, for so it has been, for time out of mind:
Into the darkness they go, the wise and the lovely. Crowned
With lilies and the laurel they go; but I am not resigned.

Lovers and thinkers, into the earth with you.
Be one with the dull, the indiscriminate dust.
A fragment of what you felt, of what you knew,
A formula, a phrase remains – but the best is lost.

The answers quick and keen, the honest look, the laughter, the love,
They are gone. They have gone to feed the roses. Elegant and curled
Is the blossom. Fragrant is the blossom. I know. But I do not approve.
More precious was the light in your eyes than all the roses in the world.

Down, down, down into the darkness of the grave
Gently they go, the beautiful, the tender, the kind;
Quietly, they go, the intelligent, the witty, the brave.
I know. But I do not approve. And I am not resigned.

DIRGE WITHOUT MUSIC *by* Edna St Vincent Millay, 1892–1950

**Effigies of Sir Ralph Green and his wife Katherine,
St Peter's Church, Lowick, Northamptonshire**

SIDE BY SIDE, their faces blurred,
The earl and countess lie in stone,
Their proper habits vaguely shown
As jointed armour, stiffened pleat,
And that faint hint of the absurd —
The little dogs under their feet.

Such plainness of the pre-baroque
Hardly involves the eye, until
It meets his left-hand gauntlet, still
Clasped empty in the other; and
One sees, with sharp tender shock,
His hand withdrawn, holding her hand.

They would not think to lie so long.
Such faithfulness in effigy
Was just a detail friends would see:
A sculptor's sweet commissioned grace
Thrown off in helping to prolong
The Latin names around the base.

They would not guess how early in
Their supine stationary voyage
Their air would change to soundless
    damage,
Turn the old tenantry away;
How soon succeeding eyes begin
To look, not read. Rigidly they

Persisted, linked, through lengths and
    breadths
Of time. Snow fell, undated. Light
Each summer thronged the grass. A bright
Litter of birdcalls strewed the same
Bone-riddled ground. And up the paths
The endless altered people came,

Washing at their identity.
Now, helpless in the hollow of
An unarmorial age, a trough
Of smoke in slow suspended skeins
Above their scrap of history,
Only an attitude remains:

Time has transfigured them into
Untruth. The stone fidelity
They hardly meant has come to be
Their final blazon, and to prove
Our almost-instinct almost true:
What will survive of us is love.

AN ARUNDEL TOMB *by* Philip Larkin, 1922–85

'FROM MY ROTTING BODY, FLOWERS SHALL GROW AND I AM IN THEM AND THAT IS ETERNITY.'

Edvard Munch, 1863–1944

WESTMACOTT Fecit 1791.

Tomb of Sir Roger Smith, St Michael's Church, Edmondthorpe, Leicestershire

SIR ROGER SMITH OF EDMONDTHORPE HALL, who died in 1655, is described on his memorial as a 'grave and religious man'. This impressive 17th-century tomb in the parish church includes the alabaster effigies of his two wives, Jane (died 1599) and Ann (died 1652). The left wrist of the lower effigy, that of Lady Ann, bears a deep-red stain. Legend says that she was a witch who had the power to transform herself into a cat. One day her butler, trying to drive this cat out of the kitchen, struck it on the paw with a meat cleaver. When the cat resumed its human form, the wound was seen on the hand of Lady Ann. After her death, this 'wounded hand' also appeared miraculously on her effigy.

The supernatural phenomena did not end here. Edmondthorpe Hall also gained an 'indelible bloodstain' on the kitchen flagstone where the cat's blood had fallen. However much the maids scrubbed, it would never disappear.

TO THE DEAR MEMORY OF VINCENT STEWART CORBET
BORN JANUARY · 27 · 1890
DIED AT ETON COLLEGE · OCTOBER · 17 · 1903

ALSO OF HIS BROTHER ROLAND JAMES CORBET
5TH BARONET · LIEUTENANT COLDSTREAM GUARDS
BORN AUGUST · 19 · 1892
DIED APRIL · 15 · 1915 ON ACTIVE SERVICE AT
GIVENCHY IN FRANCE.

ONLY THE RICHLY CARVED BASE OF THIS unusual tomb survives, the bronze statue was stolen in 1996. The inscription remembers the all too brief lives of two sons.

The ruins of the Corbet family's Elizabethan mansion can be seen from the graveyard. It was the inspiration of Sir Robert Corbet, a favourite of Elizabeth I and the building work was continued by his two sons, Robert and Vincent. It had been intended as an opulent country house modelled around the tower of an original 12th-century castle, but it was never lived in. Legend says this was because of a curse invoked on Sir Vincent Corbet by a neighbour, to whom he denied sanctuary in his hour of need. Part of the curse states '... *rejoice not in thy riches, not in the monuments of thy pride, for neither thou, nor thy children, nor thy children's children shall inherit these halls. They shall be given up to desolation; snakes, vipers and unclean beasts shall make it their refuge, and thy home shall be full of doleful creatures....*'

The building remains unfinished but the crumbling walls still bear ornate carvings of squirrels, ravens and elephants, similar to those on this memorial.

AT A YOUNG AGE JOHN FULLER (1757–1834) OF Brightling Park inherited his family's vast fortune from the manufacture of iron goods and income from sugar plantations in Jamaica. He was larger than life in every way weighing 22 stone (140 kilos), wearing his hair in a pigtail and fostering an image of eccentricity throughout his life. An outspoken Parliamentarian, he was also a controversial patron of the arts and sciences and is said to have revelled in the name 'Mad Jack Fuller'.

His legacy includes a number of extraordinary follies in the Brightling area including a temple, an observatory and a tower, many of which he had built to provide employment for the community in hard times. He arranged for the building of his own mausoleum in the shape of a pyramid some 24 years before his death. Legend says that he was entombed inside, sitting at a table wearing full evening dress, with a roast chicken and a bottle of claret to sustain him.

ONE OF THE VERY FEW EQUESTRIAN STATUES in an English church, this near life-size monument by the British sculptor Joseph Gott (1786–1860) depicts Colonel Cheney of the Royal Scots Greys at the Battle of Waterloo, 18 June 1815. He had four horses killed beneath him, but rode off on a fifth as the command of the regiment devolved to him. In later years he married Eliza Ayre whose father, John Ayre, lived at Gaddesby Hall. Colonel Cheney inherited the property where he died in 1845.

A document in the church tells the perhaps apocryphal story that Joseph Gott, on completing the statue, realised that he had left out the tongue of the dying horse, and in despair committed suicide.

Lion monument to
Richard Charles Bostock,
Abney Park Cemetery, London

Medieval stained glass,
St John the Baptist's
Church, Burford,
Oxfordshire

THOU TOO, aerial pile, whose pinnacles

Point from one shrine like pyramids on fire.

Obey'st I in silence their sweet solemn spells,

Clothing in hues of heaven thy dim and distant spire,

Around whose lessening and invisible height

Gather among the stars the clouds of night.

The dead are sleeping in their sepulchres:

And, mouldering as they sleep, a thrilling sound.

Half sense, half thought, among the darkness stirs,

Breathed from their wormy beds all living things around.

And, mingling with the still night and mute sky,

Its awful hush is felt inaudibly.

Thus solemnised and softened, death is mild

And terrorless as this serenest night.

Here could I hope, like some enquiring child

Sporting on graves, that death did hide from human sight

Sweet secrets, or besides its breathless sleep

That loveliest dreams perpetual watch did keep.

From A SUMMER EVENING CHURCHYARD, LECHLADE, GLOUCESTERSHIRE *by* Percy Bysshe Shelley, 1792–1822

Tomb of William Holland,
Kensal Green Cemetery, London

IN THE SIDE CHAPEL OF THIS LITTLE CHURCH ON the wild Cornish coastline stands the ornately carved *Mermaid's Chair* that commemorates an ancient legend. The story tells how a stranger, a beautiful and richly dressed lady, used to occasionally attend services at the church. Nobody knew where she came from and there were long intervals between her visits. All the young men of the village were attracted by her charms and one in particular, Matthew Trewella, the handsome son of the squire and the finest singer in the choir, fell in love with the seductive stranger. One day he decided to discover her identity and so after the service he followed her down to the cliffs at nearby Pendour Cove. He was never seen again.

Some years later a ship's captain saw a mermaid in a nearby cove. She complained that his ship's anchor was lying across the entrance to her home so she could not return to her lover, Matthew Trewella, and their children. The anchor was quickly raised and the captain informed the villagers of Zennor as soon as he returned to shore. They decided to carve the figure of the mermaid on the church pew as a warning to the other young men of the parish not to succumb to her wiles. She has long flowing hair and holds a comb in one hand and a mirror in the other – the symbols of heartlessness.

THE CHURCH OF ST PETER IN THE GROUNDS of historic Deene Park was originally built in the 12th century, but was extensively restored in 1868 by Lady Adeline Cardigan (1825–1915) in memory of her husband James Brudenell, 7th Earl of Cardigan (1797–1868). A committed military man, he was famous for leading the brave but tragic Charge of the Light Brigade on 25 October 1854 during the Crimean War, which was later immortalised in verse:

> Half a league, half a league,
> Half a league onward,
> All in the valley of Death
> Rode the six hundred.
> "Forward, the Light Brigade!"
> "Charge for the guns!" he said:
> Into the valley of Death
> Rode the six hundred.

> From THE CHARGE OF THE LIGHT BRIGADE
> *by* Alfred, Lord Tennyson (1809–92)

In a poignant memorial the couple's effigies lie side by side. The larger-than-life Earl had survived an unhappy marriage before falling in love with the much younger Adeline, who outlived him by 47 years. In old age she became eccentric wearing very thick make-up and outraging society by organising steeplechases through the local graveyard. She always wanted to be remembered for her beauty – even in death – and so she kept her coffin in the house and would often lie down in it and ask visitors for their opinions on her appearance.

EDMUND HARMAN (1509–1577), FROM IPSWICH, was one of Henry VIII's barbers and a gentleman of the Privy Chamber. A rich man, he acquired property in the beautiful Cotswold village of Burford and his long standing friendship with the king meant that he was the second of the eleven witnesses to Henry's will.

In the north aisle of the church Harman erected 'a monument to the Christian memory of himself and his only and most faithful wife Agnes and of the sixteen children whom by God's mercy she bore him'. The nine boys and seven girls are shown kneeling. Sadly, only two of the girls survived their parents. Another striking feature of this impressive monument is the four figures that support the long Latin inscription, which have been identified as members of an Indian tribe from South America. Why they are portrayed here is unclear, but they are believed to be the earliest representation in Britain of inhabitants of the New World.

126 **Heads, St Mary's Church,
Beverley, East Yorkshire**

THE ANCIENT 12TH-CENTURY CHURCH DEDICATED to St Aidan is all that remains of the remote moorland village of Thockrington. It was originally built by the Norman family of Umfraville and contains several tombs of the legendary Shafto family, whose former home of Bavington Hall, confiscated by the Crown for their part in the 1715 uprising, lies close by. In 1847 one of the inhabitants, a sailor, returned home from the Crimean War suffering from cholera and the infection spread rapidly throughout the village. The small population was wiped out and their homes were burnt to the ground, never to be rebuilt; only weathered tombstones recall their names.

Monument to Sophia Hume,
Countess Brownlow, by Antonia Canova.
In the foreground an effigy of
John Cust, 1st Earl Brownlow,
by Baron Carlo Marochetti.
Parish church of St Peter & St Paul,
Belton, Lincolnshire

'THERE IS BUT ONE FREEDOM, TO PUT ONESELF RIGHT
WITH DEATH. AFTER THAT EVERYTHING IS POSSIBLE.
I CANNOT FORCE YOU TO BELIEVE IN GOD. BELIEVING
IN GOD AMOUNTS TO COMING TO TERMS WITH DEATH.
WHEN YOU HAVE ACCEPTED DEATH, THE PROBLEM OF
GOD WILL BE SOLVED – AND NOT THE REVERSE.'

Albert Camus, 1913–60

Stained glass in the
Jesse window,
St Leonard's Church,
Leverington,
Cambridgeshire

'TOMORROW, AND TOMORROW, AND TOMORROW,
CREEPS IN THIS PETTY PACE FROM DAY TO DAY,
TO THE LAST SYLLABLE OF RECORDED TIME;
AND ALL OUR YESTERDAYS HAVE LIGHTED FOOLS
THE WAY TO DUSTY DEATH. OUT, OUT BRIEF CANDLE!
LIFE'S BUT A WALKING SHADOW, A POOR PLAYER
THAT STRUTS AND FRETS HIS HOUR UPON THE STAGE
AND THEN IS HEARD NO MORE: IT IS A TALE
TOLD BY AN IDIOT, FULL OF SOUND AND FURY,
SIGNIFYING NOTHING.'

From MACBETH *by* William Shakespeare, 1564–1616

138 **Table-tomb in the churchyard,**
St John the Baptist, Burford,
Oxfordshire

'But, strangest of all, the very instant the shore was touched, an immense dog sprang up on deck from below… and running forward, jumped from the bow onto the sand. Making straight for the steep cliff, where the churchyard hangs over the laneway to the East Pier… it disappeared in the darkness.'

From DRACULA *by* Bram Stoker, 1847–1912

VAMPIRES CAN TRANSFIGURE THEMSELVES into many different creatures and this description of Count Dracula's arrival at Whitby from Transylvania in the form of a dog was inspired by the Victorian author's visits to the ancient fishing village on the Yorkshire coast. In the summer evenings he would climb the 199 steps up to the clifftop and sit for hours in the old graveyard beneath the ruins of the gothic abbey. It was here, as he watched the bats circling the dark tombstones in the fading light, that his fertile imagination dreamt up perhaps the most powerful and terrifying horror story ever written.

142   **Head, Church of St Helen,**
West Keal, Lincolnshire

In AD 669 an early Saxon church was built on the south-east coast within the site of an abandoned and crumbling Roman fort that had originally been constructed to deter Saxon raiders from Europe. Today all that remains of St Mary's Church are the twin towers and several impressive tombs. In the 19th century the village surrounding the church, like the Roman fort centuries earlier, was abandoned because of coastal erosion, and the inhabitants moved inland.

A legend persists that on stormy nights the cries of babies can be heard near the church, their screams carrying on the wind. Substance was added to this folktale when archaeologists excavating the Roman fort in the 1960s found several infants' skeletons buried under the walls of the Roman barrack blocks, which are estimated to have been built between AD 200–50.

**Tomb of Charles Sackville,
5th Duke of Dorset, sculpted by
Richard Westmacott. The monument
carries the duke's cloak, shield and
coronet, with an angel holding
a text. The title became extinct
with his death.
St Peter's Church, Lowick,
Northamptonshire**

THE BELOVED AND HONOURED MEMORY OF
SACKVILLE, 5TH DUKE OF DORSET, K.G.
PARTED THIS LIFE JULY 29TH 1843,
THE 77TH YEAR OF HIS AGE.

HIS MORTAL REMAINS
O IN A VAULT UNDERNEATH THIS CHURCH,
CONTAINS THOSE OF HIS BELOVED AND ONLY BROTHER,
E GEORGE SACKVILLE GERMAIN,
HO DIED MAY 31ST 1836;
HONBLE HARRIET SACKVILLE GERMAIN, HIS WIFE,
O DIED APRIL 18TH 1835.

EVE THAT JESUS DIED AND ROSE AGAIN, EVEN SO
CH SLEEP IN JESUS WILL GOD BRING WITH HIM: I.THESS.IV.C.14.V.

THE RUINS OF A 12TH-CENTURY CHRISTIAN church stand inside the remarkably well-preserved earthworks of a Neolithic ritual henge earthwork. This is a magical site and the yew tree and blackthorn bushes only add to its timeless aura of mystery. The location of the church within the central henge at Knowlton is clear evidence of the 'Christianisation' of older pagan sites, and it is widely believed that if standing stones were a feature of the surrounding earthworks they were broken up and used in the church's construction.

Vague traces of the village of Knowlton can be found in a field to the west of the church. The community was virtually wiped out by an outbreak of bubonic plague, the Black Death, in 1485, but the church itself continued to be used up until the 18th century. There are several legends concerning the disappearance of the church's three bells – some say they were stolen, others that they were irretrievably sunk into deep pools or rivers to save them from despoilers during the Reformation. Local names such as Bell Hole or Bell Pool would seem to bear this out, as does a local rhyme:

> Knowlton bell is stole
> And thrown into White Mile Hole,
> Where all the devils in hell
> Could never pull up Knowlton Bell.

Whatever the truth, local legend claims that the bells' ghostly tolls can still be heard on moonlit nights.

REMEMBER ME when I am gone away,

Gone far away into the silent land;

When you can no more hold me by the hand,

Nor I half turn to go yet turning stay.

Remember me when no more day by day

You tell me of our future that you plann'd:

Only remember me; you understand

It will be late to counsel then or pray.

Yet if you should forget me for a while

And afterwards remember, do not grieve:

For if the darkness and corruption leave

A vestige of the thoughts that once I had,

Better by far you should forget and smile

Than that you should remember and be sad.

REMEMBER *by* Christina Rossetti, 1830–84

Stained glass by Christopher Whall, St John the Baptist's Church,
Burford, Oxfordshire

Stop all the clocks, cut off the telephone.

Prevent the dog from barking with a juicy bone,

Silence the pianos and with muffled drum

Bring out the coffin, let the mourners come.

Let aeroplanes circle moaning overhead

Scribbling on the sky the message He is Dead,

Put crêpe bows round the white necks of the public doves,

Let the traffic policemen wear black cotton gloves.

He was my North, my South, my East and West,

My working week and my Sunday rest,

My noon, my midnight, my talk, my song,

I thought that love would last forever: I was wrong.

The stars are not wanted now, put out every one;

Pack up the moon and dismantle the sun;

Pour away the ocean and sweep up the wood.

For nothing now can ever come to any good.

Funeral Blues *by* Wystan Hugh Auden, 1907–73

'FOR WHAT IS IT TO DIE,
BUT TO STAND NAKED IN THE WIND
AND MELT INTO THE SUN?'

From THE PROPHET *by* Kahil Gibran, 1883–1931

Gargoyle, Church of St Helen,
West Keal, Lincolnshire

Lindisfarne, or Holy Island, is cut off from the mainland of the wild Northumbrian coastline at high tide, and the only means of reaching the island at low tide is by a 3-mile causeway that winds through the emptiness of the mud flats that echo the call of the countless seabirds. Its tiny population is focussed around the ancient priory and a castle perched on a pinnacle of volcanic rock that overlooks the fishing harbour.

This is a place one senses must have been sacred long before AD 635 and the arrival of St Aidan. Here he created a cradle of Celtic Christianity, one of the great centres of art and learning in Europe. After St Aidan's death in AD 651, his work was kept alive by St Cuthbert, who preferred to lead a hermit's life of prayer and contemplation on one of the smaller islands. He was said to have had mysterious powers over nature and to have foretold his own death in AD 687. Eleven years later, the monks dug up his coffin to transfer his remains, but instead of finding dust and bones, discovered the body miraculously preserved. His ghost is said to haunt the priory ruins and nearby rocks.

164 **The Causeway, Holy Island,
Lindisfarne, Northumberland**

Blount memorial, Church of St John the Baptist, Kinlet, Shropshire

O NE OF THE FINEST ELIZABETHAN MONUMENTS in England, this memorial dates from 1581 and the effigies commemorate Sir George Blount (1513–81), his wife Constantia and their children, John and Dorothy. The boy died young, choking to death on an apple core, and his sister, against her father's wishes, married a local man of poor social standing who had previously insulted Sir George. In a rage he put a curse on her and all her descendants.

Below the effigies on the monument is one of a cadaver, the representation of the dead body of Sir George as was the custom of the time. But legend says that Sir George's spirit did not rest for long. His ghost came back to haunt the house and grounds with such frequency and ferocity that the old hall had to be abandoned and a new house built in 1720. However the manifestations still continued and finally priests were summoned to exorcise his spirit and bring peace to both him and those he haunted. In a strange ceremony they read verses from an ancient book of magic and succeeded in capturing Squire Blount's spirit in a glass bottle. They stoppered the bottle securely and carried it to the church where they placed it by his tomb. There it remained undisturbed until the end of the 19th century as no local person dared to touch it but then the bottle must have been stolen or broken – releasing Squire Blount's restless ghost to wander abroad again.

THE GREEN MAN, HIS FACE SHROUDED IN foliage, with branches and vines sprouting from his mouth and nose, many bearing fruit or birds, stares down at us from the roofs, pillars and doorways of many of our churches and cathedrals. This enigmatic symbol can be found in countries and cultures around the world on Roman columns in Turkey to Jain Temples in Rajasthan and dates back into the mists of time. He is primarily interpreted as a symbol of our 'oneness with the earth', of rebirth or 'renaissance', representing the cycle of growth being reborn anew each spring. But there are others who see this ancient pagan symbol as a representation of the horned god or devil, a mixture of the Celtic god Cernunnos and the Greek god Pan. The medieval church is said to have seen the figure as a reminder of man's fragile existence — a warning that he is powerless in the face of nature as it slowly envelopes him.

The Sutton Benger Green Man is considered to be one of the finest examples of a foliate head sculpture in existence. He is surrounded by hawthorn leaves in which birds and berries abound. His face has an almost melancholic, sinister expression of acceptance as he waits and watches us, as the past always watches — foretelling mortality.